Swiss Family Robinson

Johann Wyss

Swiss Family Robinson

Many years ago, lots of families left Europe to look for new homes. They needed land to farm and wanted a better life for their children. Swiss Family Robinson is about a father, a mother and their four children. They decide to leave their home in Switzerland. The four sons are 14, 12, 10 and 7 years old. The family is sailing to a new country when a terrible storm begins...

The father decides to write the story of their adventure. He hopes other people will learn from it.

Shipwreck

The wind blew day and night. The sea tossed our ship up and down. After six days everyone was tired and frightened. My poor children stayed close to their mother. I looked at their white faces. What could I do to help them?

Then, with joy, I heard someone shout, 'Land! Land!' But suddenly there was a loud crash. Water poured in and the ship began to sink.

'Lower the boats!' the Captain shouted above the noise of the storm. 'We're going to drown!' But the frightened sailors forgot us. In the dark and the rain I saw there were no boats left.

During the night, the storm began to calm down. The ship did not sink and at last my children slept in the cabin.

In the morning there was blue sky above. I climbed out of the cabin and saw that the cabin end of the ship was stuck between two high rocks. We were above the water and I could see land.

Soon my wife and sons woke up. The boys were surprised that we were alone. 'Have the sailors gone?' they asked. 'Have they taken away the boats? Oh, Father, why did they leave us behind? What can we do by ourselves?'

But Fritz, my eldest son, soon had an idea. The sea was sparkling in the sun. 'Look,' he said, 'the sea will soon be calm. We can swim to the shore.'

'That's fine for you,' said Ernest. 'You and Father are good swimmers, but think of Mother and the rest of us.'

'I know!' said Jack. He was only ten years old but he was very brave. 'We will make a raft.'

'A good idea,' I said, 'but it will be difficult. First we must look for useful things.'

Ernest found a hammer, some nails and lots of tools. Fritz and I looked for wood. Franz, the youngest boy, went with his mother. They came back with food and some good news. A cow, a donkey, some goats, sheep and hens were alive. I was not so pleased with Jack. He had two large, hungry dogs. 'Oh, please Father, let me keep them!' he said. 'They will be useful. They will help us to hunt when we reach land.' I had to agree.

We spent all day making a raft. It was very hard work but at last it was ready. We were all tired and it was late so we slept for one more night on the ship.

Safe on land

Early the next morning we put food, clothes, carpenters' tools, guns, fishing rods, pots and other useful things on the raft. We made swimming belts for the larger animals, then pushed off from the ship and rowed towards the shore.

I looked for a safe place to land. The cliffs were very high. We could see only rock and stone.

'This will help,' said Jack as he took a telescope from his pocket.

'Look,' said Fritz, 'palm trees!'

I put the telescope to my eye.

'What can you see?' they all wanted to know.

'Fritz is right. Those are coconut palms. There is a stream, too. It flows out to the sea and the land is flat. It will be easy to get ashore there.'

The dogs ran up the beach ahead of us. Some penguins that lived there made a lot of noise when they saw us!

We took everything off the raft before we tied it up. I made a fireplace with some flat stones and the boys made a pile of sticks. Then I filled an iron pot with water and soon my wife and Franz were cooking soup over the fire.

Fritz took a gun and crossed the stream. Ernest did not like walking so he sat on the beach. Jack climbed over the rocks, looking for fish. I began to make a tent.

Suddenly I heard Jack shouting for help. I ran to where he was standing in a deep rock pool. A huge crab had its front claws around his leg. I held the back of the crab and at last Jack pulled himself free.

We had crab for dinner. It was delicious! Afterwards we slept on the ground, on the soft grass under our tent. It was our first night in a strange land.

Happy to be alive

The sun woke my wife and me early in the morning. We talked and made plans while the children slept.

'Do you think all the other people on the ship drowned?' I asked. 'First, we must look for other people. We will also try to find out where we are.'

'Take Fritz with you,' my wife said, 'and a gun. I will stay here with the younger children.'

Fritz and I went to explore. We took a dog with us and walked all morning. The sun was hot. We noticed lots of fruits on the trees and I told Fritz some of their names.

Suddenly we heard a strange noise. Fritz ran ahead with his gun. The dog had found a baby monkey. We looked up and saw more monkeys in the palm trees. They began to throw coconuts at us!

I showed Fritz how to open a coconut and we drank the milk.

'How do you know about these things?' asked Fritz.

'I learned about them from reading travel books,' I told him.

We climbed a steep hill. From the top we could see a long way.
The sea and some small islands lay on one side. On the other,
we could see mountains and valleys, but there were no people.
We rested and then walked back to our camp.

When we got back, the others ran to meet us. 'Have you found
anything interesting?' they asked.

We showed them the coconuts and some fruits. Fritz was
carrying the baby monkey.

'This is a beautiful country,' I told my wife, 'but no one lives
here. We are all by ourselves.'

We were all alone but we were very happy to be alive.

A new home

The weather was still good. I decided to return to the wreck before there was another storm. We needed all the useful things from the ship. Fritz came with me and we worked hard. We went every day for a week.

My wife stayed with the other children. I did not like leaving her alone at our camp, so she made a flag from a white sail. It was a signal. We could see the flag from the wreck. If there was any danger, she would lower the flag.

The ship was carrying many things for people in a new country. We found clothes, furniture, food and seeds. There were tools, wheels, matches and rope. There was even a yacht! It was in pieces but we put it together. We were lucky to have so many things.

One day my wife met us at the landing place. She was very excited. 'I want to show you something,' she said.

We crossed the stream. The younger boys started to run ahead along the path towards some woods. 'Follow us!' they shouted.

They took us to a place with huge trees. 'Look,' said my wife, 'isn't it beautiful here? It is too hot by the sea. Here it is cool. I want to build a house in the trees.'

I agreed at once. But how could we carry all our things there? First we had to make a bridge over the stream. Jack chose a good place. The cow and the donkey pulled the heavy wood from the beach.

'How can we find out if our wood is long enough to reach across?' I asked.

'We can use some string,' said Ernest. 'Tie one end to a stone and throw it across. Mark it, then pull it back and measure it against the log.'

I followed my son's good idea. At last we had a bridge. I made a cart, too, with wood and wheels from the wreck.

It took many weeks to build our house but all the boys loved helping. First we made a floor about ten metres above the ground. Then we cut down some branches and built walls and a strong roof. We climbed a rope ladder up to our tree house and hung our hammocks from the higher branches.

'The roof and walls are very strong,' I said. 'Even a big bear would find it hard to break in.'

My wife was very pleased. 'It will be cool in hot weather,' she said. 'It is beautiful. I love our new home.'

We were safe and warm at last.

Daily life

And so our days passed. We were not homesick for we had already decided to leave Switzerland and start a new life. We had not chosen to be alone, but a few people more or less did not matter.

We took everything from the shipwreck. We even had beds, so we did not have to sleep on the ground or in hammocks any more. We had the animals from the ship and found many more on the land. We planted trees and seeds and found sugar and potatoes. We had good food to eat.

We were busy all day. My wife made butter and cheese from the cow's milk. She planted a garden of flowers and vegetables around our tree house. Every day we looked after the animals and the fields and everyone helped to build new huts and barns.

We took time to rest and the boys had time to play, too. The sea was warm so they swam a lot. They were good swimmers. They dived from the rocks into the clear, blue water. They climbed and ran and jumped. They were strong and healthy.

All the children had pets. Fritz found a young eagle and he gave the baby monkey to Ernest. Jack had his two dogs, and soon they had puppies.

'If I had a pony, I could go riding every day,' said Franz.

Then Fritz's eagle found some huge eggs. They were ostrich eggs and soon Franz had a pet ostrich. It was not long before he could ride his ostrich every day.

Then, one day, the weather changed. There were clouds in the sky and the wind started to blow. The sky got dark. Then it began to rain. For weeks we had to stay in the tree house. My wife sewed. Ernest drew pictures of the birds, animals and plants he had seen. Fritz and Jack taught Franz to read. We all liked music. My wife played the guitar and we all sang together. And I began to write about our life here.

Thanksgiving

On the day we reached land, I had made a mark with my knife on a tree. I had marked the tree every day since then.

During dinner one evening I said to my family, 'My dears, do you know that tomorrow is a very important day? We shall call it Thanksgiving Day. We have lived here for one year.'

Everyone was surprised to hear this. The time had passed very quickly.

We had a wonderful day. There were games to play. The boys ran races and won prizes. I set the table with our best things. My wife cooked delicious food and made a cake. We talked about everything that had happened since the storm a year before.

We were very happy. But a few weeks later, something frightened us. We were all under the trees. Fritz and I were reading. My wife was sewing and the younger children were jumping and playing. Suddenly Fritz jumped up.

'I see something, Father! What can it be? It is coming towards the bridge.' He looked through the telescope, then passed it to me. 'It looks like a snake, doesn't it?'

It was a snake. A huge snake, ten metres long. It was very frightening. As I watched, it lifted its head about five metres

from the ground. We were in danger! We all climbed quickly up into our tree house. Our legs were shaking.

At last the snake disappeared into the long grass near the stream. We slept badly that night.

The next day Fritz and I took our guns out with us. We were still frightened but we had to find the snake. When at last we found it, we shot the snake dead.

Rescue

Year followed year. We called our country New Switzerland. Our farm covered many acres of land. We built a new house of stone and rock for the winter and in the summer we lived in our tree house.

Fritz was now 24 years old. Ernest was 22 and Jack was 20. Even Franz was no longer a child. He was 17 years old. They could all look after themselves very well.

One day Fritz told me that he had a plan. He wanted to find out if we lived on an island. He took lots of food and a tent and set off in his boat. He was going to try to sail round the island.

Every day I looked through my telescope. At last I saw him. He was safely home again. He had a big box full of pearls and he had an interesting story to tell.

Fritz had travelled for many days. He saw many small islands. Then he came to a coral reef where many sea birds lived. They began to fly at his boat. A very large bird hit the sail and fell on to the boat. It was an albatross and round its leg Fritz found a piece of paper. Someone had written, in English, 'Save me from the smoking rock'. Fritz tore a piece of cloth from the sail and wrote on it, 'Help is near'. He tied it round the bird's leg and then let it fly away again.

We were all excited. Did someone else live near us? We decided we must go and look.

Fritz led the way in his boat. We followed in our yacht. Five days later we saw smoke above the trees on a small island. We sailed closer. Someone waved from the beach. We had found a shipwrecked girl! We took her back to our home.

The girl's name was Jenny Montrose. Three years ago she was sailing home to England when there was a terrible storm and the ship sank. Jenny was alone on her island.

During the winter Jenny taught us all to speak English well. Then, one day Jack and Franz were cleaning their guns. They fired and we heard a ship's guns fire back from a long way off!

Fritz and I set off in the boat. An hour later we passed some cliffs and there, in the bay, was an English ship. We went back to tell the family. We all put on our best clothes then sailed to the bay in our yacht. When we saw the ship we shouted and waved. The sailors saw us and were very surprised.

The Captain had come to look for Jenny. Now we could all go home. But my wife and I loved New Switzerland. We would miss our life here, so we decided to stay. Ernest and Jack decided to stay too. Some people on the ship asked to live in New Switzerland with us and we agreed at once.

A few days later, we said goodbye to Franz, Fritz and Jenny. I gave Fritz my book with the story of our adventures. My wife and I watched and waved from the beach as the ship sailed away. We knew our sons would return one day.

The writer

The story of the Swiss family Robinson is by a Swiss man called Johann David Wyss. He lived in Switzerland about 200 years ago and had four sons, like the man in the story. He was a clever man and read lots of books. He enjoyed *Robinson Crusoe*, a famous English story about a shipwrecked man who lived alone on a desert island. He liked to tell stories to his own children. Many years later, one son found the stories in a notebook. He asked his father to make them into a book. People loved the book and it was soon printed in many different languages.

'Lessons' from the book

Johann Wyss taught his children many things by telling them exciting stories. They listened to *Swiss Family Robinson* and learned about plants and animals, about how to make things, how things work and how to look after themselves. Here are some 'lessons' from the book.

Animals

Johann Wyss describes many animals in the book. Do you know this animal?

> 'It is as large as a sheep. Its head is like a mouse. It has long ears. It has a tail like a tiger's. It looks as if it is sitting up. Its back legs are very strong. Its front legs are very short. It jumps and moves very fast.'

Making bread

The father of the Swiss family Robinson was not a baker. He had no wheat flour or yeast. He had no oven. But he decided to make bread. This is how he did it.

Ernest saw the monkey dig up a root and eat it. Then he took one of the roots to his father.

'I know this root,' his father said. 'In some countries they make bread from it.'

First he made a fire, then he put an iron plate on the fire to get hot. He washed the root then rubbed it over some rough metal. The root broke up and it looked a bit like flour. He mixed it with water to make a dough, then he kneaded it. He shaped the dough into a loaf and baked the loaf on the hot plate. It smelt delicious!

Lifting and moving things

The family made a raft to get off the wrecked ship. They finished it but they could not move it. 'I must have a lever,' said the father.

They cut logs. They put one end of a long piece of wood under the front of the raft. The father pulled down on the other end of the piece of wood and he lifted the front of the raft. Then the children put the logs under the raft as rollers. Now when they pushed, the raft moved over the rollers.

Ernest asked his father how they did it. 'When you used the piece of wood,' he said, 'you lifted the raft. How did you do that alone? When we all tried together at first, it did not move!'

His father explained how a lever works.

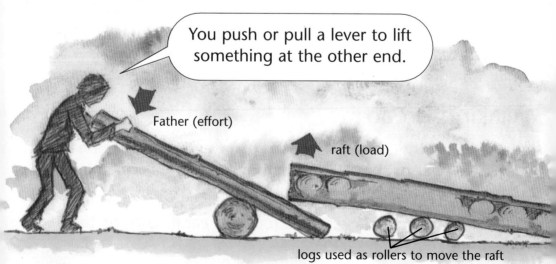

You push or pull a lever to lift something at the other end.

Father (effort)

raft (load)

logs used as rollers to move the raft

Questions

What can you remember about the story?

1 What country does the family come from?

2 Who is the oldest child? Who is the youngest?

3 How old was Jack when the ship was wrecked?

4 Name four kinds of animal they found on the ship.

5 How did they move things from the beach to the tree house?

6 How long did Franz and Fritz live in New Switzerland?

7 How long did Jenny stay on the island alone?

8 How do you think these people felt when they said goodbye at the end?   a the father   b Fritz

9 How does a baker make bread? How is it different from the Swiss family Robinson's bread?

10 How did they move the raft from the ship?

Answer: The animal described on page 29 is a kangaroo.

31

Macmillan Education
Between Towns Road, Oxford OX4 3PP
A division of Macmillan Publishers Limited
Companies and representatives throughout the world

www.macmillan.com
ISBN-10: 0-333-67502-9
ISBN-13: 978-0-3336-7502-1

First published 1998

Illustrated by Gillian Hunt/Specs Art

Printed and bound in Egypt by Zamzam Presses

2007 2006
14   13   12